Semrad

The Heart
of a
Therapist

ABOUT THE EDITORS

Susan Rako attended Wellesley College and graduated from Albert Einstein College of Medicine in 1966. After completing two years of residency in psychiatry at the Massachusetts Mental Health Center under Dr. Elvin Semrad and a year of adult and child psychiatry at the Beth Israel Hospital in Boston, she became Staff Psychiatrist at the Massachusetts Mental Health Center and (part-time) Clinical Instructor in Psychiatry at Harvard Medical School. Dr. Rako practices psychiatry and teaches a psychotherapeutic seminar in Newton, Massachusetts.

Harvey Mazer, a graduate of Harvard University and Albert Einstein College of Medicine, received his psychiatric training at the Massachusetts Mental Health Center under Dr. Elvin Semrad (1965-1968). He has completed fellowships in adolescent and university psychiatry at MIT and Harvard and is now Consultant Psychiatrist for the Brandeis University Psychological Counseling Center. Dr. Mazer is engaged in the private practice of psychotherapy in Cambridge and Lexington, Massachusetts.

Semrad

The Heart of a Therapist

edited by
Susan Rako, M.D.
and
Harvey Mazer, M.D.

Jason Aronson Inc.
Northvale, New Jersey
London

Fourth Printing 1988

ISBN: 0-87668-684-6

Library of Congress Catalog Number: 84-45091

Manufactured in the United States of America.

Psychoanalysis is the study of self-deception.
—Sigmund Freud

I've always thought that some of the things
people suffer most from are the things they
tell themselves that are not true.
—Elvin Semrad

Acknowledgments

We are grateful for material shared and contributions of quotations or anecdotes sent by:

Cori Altman, ACSW, Joseph I. Bernstein, M.D., Herbert N. Brown, M.D., Abram Chipman, Ph.D., Samuel Epstein, M.D., Pattison Esmiol, M.D., Linda Fleger-Berman, ACSW, Barry Gault, M.D., Thomas G. Gutheil, M.D., J. Allan Hobson, M.D., Fay Linden, ACSW, William Lutnicki, Charles Magraw, M.D., Doris Menzer-Benaron, M.D., Jeremy Nahum, M.D., Timothy M. Ravinus, M.D., Harry L. Senger, M.D., David Speigel, M.D., William Stage, M.D., Rachel Wheeler, and John Zinner, M.D.

In appreciation for their enthusiastic encouragement we wish to thank Irwin Avery, M.D., Max Day, M.D., Judith Huizenga, M.D., Aaron Kaye, D.M.D., Linda Herman Land, MSW, David Levi, M.D., Ann Mandell, M.A., and Martin Miller, M.D.

In addition there are special people to whom we owe particular thanks:

Mrs. Hulda Tracy, whose typing of the original material from long-hand scribbled notes was essential to the beginning of our work.

William Stage, M.D., for permission to use the candid photograph of Dr. Semrad on the dust jacket.

Cori Altman, ACSW, for her substantial and sensitive help in editing the introductory material and for sharing in the growth and development of this book from its inception.

Linda Fleger-Berman, ACSW, for her discriminating opinions and support.

Michael Farrin, who copy edited the book, and Bruce Elwell, who supervised production, for their skill and forbearance.

Jason Aronson, M.D., for believing in the value of this project and for cooperating to make the literal publication of this book possible.

We wish to express our gratitude to our families: Jennifer Rako, and Benjamin, Jennifer, and Deena Mazer, for their specific help and general patience with this project.

We feel that our collaboration has been fruitful; the book could not have been completed without the particular style and contributions of each.

Contents

Introduction

On October 7, 1976, news that Dr. Elvin Semrad had suffered a sudden and fatal heart attack spread rapidly and painfully through the Boston psychiatric community. With his death at age sixty-seven, we suffered the loss of an extraordinarily gifted clinician and teacher, loved and respected by generations of colleagues and students.

As a training analyst and former president of the Boston Psychoanalytic Institute, professor of psychiatry at Harvard Medical School, lecturer at several colleges and schools of social work, and Clinical Director in charge of psychiatric residency training at the Massachusetts Mental Health Center for more than twenty years, Dr. Semrad had become the most influential teacher of psychiatry in the Boston area and one of the most important teachers of his generation.

He was a "psychiatrist's psychiatrist," an "analyst's analyst," and his unique approach to his work was incorporated as welcome sustenance by many of those who learned from him. We—hundreds of his former students—now practice and teach psychiatry in offices, clinics, and medical schools throughout the United States and abroad. It is likely that Dr. Semrad is quoted or paraphrased regularly by many of us, since what he said and the way he said it went to the heart of the fundamental and difficult matters that concern therapists and patients.

Elvin Semrad authored and coauthored more than two hundred papers, with substantial work on treatment of the psychoses and group psychotherapy. But these writings were often "works of the head"—complex, theoretical, and not invitingly readable. By contrast, Dr. Semrad's genius bloomed on personal contact—when he *sat* with a patient, a student, or a group, made heart-to-heart contact, and shared an occasional comment.

Experienced psychiatrists and trainees alike would look forward to the conferences he chaired as the high point of their week. There we saw his patience, warmth, respect for others, and his deep commitment to the necessity for people to make their own decisions. We saw his gentle firmness and his ability to expose and explore the heart of many a central but elusive matter, using words and allusions that connected with people's unconscious and primary process. He demonstrated the importance he placed on loss and lost objects in life, and on the need to grieve these losses adequately in order to go on. He believed in the possibilities of man and in the primacy of feeling. He recognized the common use of self-deception as an avoidance of pain. He believed in the importance of being able to acknowledge reality, grapple with it and bear it, and put it into perspective in order to deal with life and to grow. He had a special ability to simplify the complex, to recognize, identify, and describe the feelings common to people, and to communicate this in his clinical work and teaching.

Elvin Semrad was born August 10, 1909 in Abie, Nebraska. He was reared in the same area, cherished this country background, and loved to refer to himself as "just a hayseed from Nebraska." After graduating from Peru State Teachers College, he went to Nebraska Medical School and interned in psychiatry at Omaha. He came to Boston in 1935, at the age of twenty-six, where he completed three years of residency under Dr. Macfie Campbell, a significant contributor to descriptive psychiatry, at the old Boston Psychopathic Hospital, now the Massachusetts Mental Health Center. Dr. Semrad spent a final psychiatric residency year at McLean Hospital, with Dr. John Whitehorn, pursuing his particular interest in the treatment of psychosis. From 1938 to 1942 he was a graduate assistant in neurology in the outpatient department of the Massachusetts General Hospital. He began analytic training at the Boston Psychoanalytic Institute, left to serve in the army during World War II, returned to graduate from the Institute in March 1948, and remained in Boston after that. Dr. Semrad worked for six years training psychiatric residents at the Boston State Hospital before becoming Clinical Director at the Massachusetts Mental Health Center, where, in 1965 and 1966, we first met him.

As medical students considering psychiatric residency training, we and others had learned that the Massachusetts Mental Health Center, a small, 140-bed state mental hospital affiliated with Harvard Medical School, was an institution that offered an exceptional program in analytically oriented psychotherapy. The staff was heavily weighted with psychoanalysts at a time when psychoanalysis had attained preeminence among the psychotherapies. The patient population was selected particularly for potential ability to benefit from psychotherapy. About twenty-five first-year residents, chosen from hundreds of applicants, had the experience of working intensively with a manageable caseload. Daily teaching conferences and seven to eight hours weekly of individual supervision encouraged depth of understanding and psychodynamic formulation. Dr. Semrad's humanistic clinical orientation and training philosophy formed the basis of the teaching and treatment program

Dr. Semrad himself was "staff visit" at four weekly conferences, supervised first-year residents weekly in groups of two, and taught elective seminars to second and third year residents. He also met daily with the chief residents, and was accessible, office door ajar, for impromptu consultation. In order to be available, he scheduled his own patients early and late, worked Saturdays, and seemed to have time for anyone who needed him.

Dr. Semrad believed that the most significant learning came "from the seat of your pants"; that "the patient is the only textbook we require." He felt that the best treatment was one person helping another to look at the facts of his life. He emphasized that the first and most important task of the neophyte psychotherapist was to learn to *sit* with the patient, to listen to and to hear him, and to help him to stand the pain he could not bear alone.

Dr. Semrad's humanism and insistence upon understanding was balanced at the Massachusetts Mental Health Center by the no-nonsense, action-oriented administrative style of Dr. Jack Ewalt, superintendent of the hospital. Dr. Ewalt ran the hospital, made decisions, and made sure things got done; Dr. Semrad's main function was to help people learn.

The following individual reminiscences may provide the reader a sense of how each of us came to collect the quotations that we have since pooled in compiling and editing this volume:

Harvey Mazer, M.D.

During my first contacts with Dr. Semrad, when I was a beginning resident, I was immediately impressed by his way with patients, his feeling for what lay in a person's heart, and the deep sense of truth and power that pervaded his simple, uncomplicated words. His language stood in marked contrast to the analytic jargon often used by the other supervisors. His comments frequently produced that sense of revelation cartoonists have depicted as a lightbulb flashing above the head; with a single illuminating remark he could place an issue in dramatic relief.

I was fascinated by this man, who at times would say nothing, leaving us to figure things out for ourselves. At other times he would make a few brief statements that sounded either brilliant or so vague, general, and simplistic that it wasn't clear whether they had any meaning at all. Occasionally I wondered whether he had lifted them directly from the *Reader's Digest*. Was he an amazing guru, or a fake? I didn't know, but decided to begin writing down what he said so that I could re-read it later and think more about it, so that his words would not disappear like smoke.

Over the next three years of my residency, I arranged to have as much contact with Dr. Semrad as I could, feeling that he was the most important teacher at "The Psycho." I attended his conferences, requested him as my supervisor, took a seminar with him, and finally, as a chief resident, participated in a daily staff meeting with him. I invited him to our service for consultation as often as possible. All this time, I recorded what he said with continuing interest.

My first reaction to Dr. Semrad had been to develop a strong positive transference. He represented the idealized "good, wise, all-knowing, all-loving, all-accepting" father. Only as I had more contact with him did I gradually develop a more realistic sense of Elvin Semrad, the man. I learned that, indeed, he wasn't perfect. I began to notice his obesity, his heavy smoking, his habitual lateness for appointments, his frustrating passivity at times, his long hours of overwork, and what seemed a constant sense of sadness underlying his smile. He seemed to display a certain pessimism about life.

Though I could see imperfections and began to read apparent inconsistencies within the volume of notes I was accumulating, I realized that the more I knew Dr. Semrad, the more I liked him. In fact, by the end of the residency I felt a strong love for him. He was an unusually empathic man who had a special ability to provoke intense curiosity and feeling. He was able to capture in a few straightforward words complicated and important concepts; he stimulated me and others to do our own personal work of learning.

I learned more about being a psychotherapist from Elvin Semrad than I have learned from anyone else in my life. What he taught was not theoretical. By example, he taught respect for people and for life. He demonstrated how to sit with people and their pain—to listen, to hear, and to sort out what mattered to them. He showed how to help them look at their lives in a way that would enable them to find their own solutions to their difficulties.

Saying good-bye to Dr. Semrad at the end of my residency, I mentioned to him that sometime in the future I might like to publish the comments he had seen me scribbling down during the past three years. His response, typical of him, was: "I hope you will take away with you what you found valuable, use it, and pass it on. As for the rest, throw it away!"

Susan Rako, M.D.

On October 15, 1976, I spoke informally at the memorial service for Dr. Semrad at the Massachusetts Mental Health Center, where I had trained as a medical student in 1966, as a psychiatric resident beginning in 1967, and where I had been teaching since 1970. I shared with staff and patients some of Dr. Semrad's comments that I had recorded in a small notebook from the beginning of my residency. After the memorial service, Dr. George Ainslie's suggestion that I compile a volume of the quotations to be more widely shared encouraged me to contact Dr. Mazer, who I knew had independently recorded hundreds of Dr. Semrad's comments. We decided to collaborate in order to create this book.

My notebook of sayings was begun in July of 1967, when we of the Day Hospital Service of the Massachusetts Mental Health Center crammed into Dr. Semrad's office for the first of our weekly Wednesday morning conferences, to present a patient and a therapist to him. Some of the quoted comments are remarks Dr. Semrad made to the patient; other comments he made to the therapist only after asking the patient, "May I have your permission to talk to your doctor about your problem?"

I wrote the words down exactly as I heard them. Reviewing them now, out of context, many of them have a powerful sense of universal relevance.

It wasn't then nor is it now my way to record much of anything. I have never collected the words of anyone else in writing. But I knew when I first sat with Dr. Semrad that I wanted his company on the strange, exciting, frightening, frustrating, and lonely road I had chosen to travel.

One of the things he said was, "The most important function of a human being is to make up his mind what's for him and what's not for him." I was fortunate to know clearly in my mind, my heart, and my body that to be an analytic therapist was for me; to listen to what Dr. Semrad had to say and to write some of it down was for me.

His simple statements had a peculiar power, an immediate familiarity which reminded me of the experience of reclaiming repressed memories— thoughts and feelings newly available, but bearing the sense of always having been known. His plain talk often brought a pulse of recognition, a sense of shared experience. He allowed the impression *that he had been there*, wherever, or that he would readily go, using the man or the woman in himself, as he would say. And there he sat, in his amplitude, very often smiling mischievously, teasingly, wisely, kindly, enigmatically, diabolically, attesting to the safety of taking life on, simply—of acknowledging, bearing, and finally putting into perspective the feelings that went with the living of it. "We're just big messes trying to help bigger messes, and the only reason we can do it is that we've been through it before, and have survived."

On the door of his office, which I experienced as the heart of the hospital, Dr. Semrad had a timeworn, hand-inked note which read:

> When door is ajar *come in*.
> When closed, am busy.
> If emergency, Please knock.

That note on the door was an ingenious facilitator. It demonstrated the importance Dr. Semrad placed both on being accessible and on being clear as to the terms of that accessibility. The door was very often open. After I completed formal training, my custom was to stop in to talk to him every few months, as did others, on staff or away, who enjoyed this casual and special contact.

He was an extraordinary resource: a source of names of therapists (often former students) for my patients when they moved out of state, and a source of consultation when therapy seemed to be stuck. Just knowing that he was there to support the "hanging in" was often support enough without the actual consultation. He appeared never to doubt the capacity of a patient or of a therapist to grow, and his nonintrusive help was steadily dependable. To use his words, he would help the therapist "keep working and not go through these periods of being as stymied as the patient"; he would help the therapist "not to go dead."

Give and take between Dr. Semrad and me occurred simply and naturally, comfortably within the "distance for living" established between us—a distance marked in one aspect by our always addressing one another as Dr. Rako and Dr. Semrad. He was a genius at balancing formality and intimacy. His avoidance of *tutoyer* and his use of formal language allowed an extraordinary amount of safe openness. He could talk with patients more effectively about more difficult material than anyone else I have known.

These introductory pages contain several references to the fundamental importance that Dr. Semrad placed on attending to the sadness and losses of one's life. Indeed, the lessons about sadness that I learned "at his knee" have been of essential and sustaining use to me in practicing psychotherapy and in living my life. When I came more into my own as a therapist, I needed also to learn more about joy, anger, and aggression, and he was of less help with these. In addition, I was at times disappointed and frustrated at Dr. Semrad's choice to maintain a certain aloof distance and to avoid engaging in vigorous dialogue about clinical and theoretical issues.

He was not all and everything, but he was very much. As my teacher, he let me use him as I needed—and by example taught me to try to help my patients in that way: "A therapist is a kind of service man. There are so many things a patient can want to use you for—and if you can swallow your own ideas of how things *should* be, you can perform a real service."

Editors' Note

To some extent this project has been part of our own grieving, as we continue to mourn Dr. Semrad and to put him and his teaching into perspective in our lives. His death, as he might have said, "left a hole in our hearts." It is also meant as a tribute to him—to share, with others who knew him and who miss him, some of what we have left of him. And as a wish to give to people who have not had the chance to know him a sense of what he was like—what he believed in and what he taught.

We did not want to produce a detailed life history; neither did we want to write a philosophical presentation of his theoretical position or a critique of his beliefs. We chose rather to let his comments stand for themselves, as they did during his life. He never explained them but left them for others to interpret and to use, and we have done the same.

Our sampling of Dr. Semrad's extemporaneous comments provides a sense of him as teacher and clinician. Of course the material in this book does not represent his complete thought or feeling on any subject. His remarks often touch only one side of a matter, as he tried to make a particular point in a teaching context. In addition, we wish it to be known that there is no point-to-point correspondence between Dr. Semrad's ideas and attitudes and our own.

During our years of residency at the Massachusetts Mental Health Center—1965 through 1969—we independently recorded, longhand and verbatim, nearly all the quotations printed here. The topics that Dr. Semrad emphasized and reemphasized stood out clearly as we reviewed our material. We have divided the book into sections reflecting the topics he commented on most often.

Many of his remarks can not be neatly categorized. Our placements are therefore necessarily somewhat arbitrary. It seems more fitting than arbitrary, however, that those included in the "Therapy" section are virtually interchangeable with those dealing with the various aspects of life, since Dr. Semrad believed that doing psychotherapy was essentially a process of helping a person attend carefully to the facts and feelings of his life.

With regard to the editing: in order to preserve the particular rhythm of

Dr. Semrad's speech, we have tried to avoid changing syntax, grammar, or wording. We have also attempted to use punctuation to this end as much as possible, with relative disregard for formal rules. We have changed a few unusually awkward quotations to make them understandable out of context.

Several quotes and anecdotes were recounted or sent to us by colleagues, patients, and former students of Dr. Semrad. Since many of these were recalled from memory by the persons who sent them, the wording and syntax may not be exact. Where such a quote sounds like Semrad, we have included it.

Our work on this book has given us a better defined and more fully developed appreciation of Dr. Semrad, the man and teacher. We are thankful that we were able to work with and learn from him.

S.R.
H.M.

The Body

What is there in life if you can't feel it in your body: love, joy, sadness, despair.

* * *

The most important part of the integration of a personality is to make peace with one's own body and be at home with it.

* * *

The first object you love or hate is your own body. You love it when it feels good and hate it when it feels bad. It feels good when it's held, and bad when it's causing pain. When we hurt we hold ourselves, don't we?

* * *

Everybody has to buy peace between her head and the rest of her.

* * *

Does your heart believe your head? Ask your heart.

* * *

Anything below genital level is body to body reaction. This is why men have such trouble becoming therapists. They can't accept their pregenital states, that they're just human beings with body feelings.

* * *

As a sexual experience proceeds, the debatable issues go on until the head gives in entirely to the body. In even the ordinary sexual excitement that people permit themselves, and most people don't permit themselves a hell of a lot, consciousness goes out the window.

Feeling

The most important part of a person's life is his affect.

* * *

If you feel like crying, you cry. You see, there's one thing you can depend on, and that's the autonomic nervous system. It never lies. It's so far from the head it doesn't even know there is a head.

* * *

The one thing all people have is feelings—their actions and thoughts are often means of disguising these feelings from themselves.

* * *

What one feels is an aspect of life not amenable to reason.

* * *

To truly communicate with people is to communicate with their feelings, usually in terms of their
body feelings.

* * *

No one can hide his feelings forever. There comes a
day of reckoning when one has to face his feelings.

* * *

When you feel nothing: *that*'s when you hurt most.

* * *

How can thoughts control the world when they
have only words to work with, and the feelings are all
in the heart?

* * *

There are two basic emotions—sadness and anxiety. The others are reactions to these: sadness that we can't have what we want; anxiety that we can't *let* ourselves have what we want.

* * *

Sadness is a *real* emotion; you cannot escape how the body feels.

* * *

If you have somebody to be mad at, then there's a place for all the energy to go.

* * *

After all, how many things do people get enraged and frustrated about? Either there's an obstacle in their course that they can't get around, or they can't get someone to love them as much as they want to be loved.

* * *

On Feelings: First they have to be acknowledged, then one has to bear them, and finally one has to decide what to do with them.

Love

Falling in love is the only socially acceptable psychosis.

* * *

All men scheme to get their ideal woman, and all women scheme to get their ideal man. Sometimes they do it in such a subtle and sophisticated way that it's not even conscious. They call it "love." Nobody *thinks* when they're in love. If they did, the honeymoon would be over. Don't get me wrong. I'm not against it. I got hooked myself. I don't know who started it. I just observe it as it happens.

* * *

Love is the standard issue; only the objects change.

* * *

Love is love, no matter how you slice it. A touch of love is like a touch of pregnancy.

* * *

People in love just live it; they never define it—
because if they defined it, it wouldn't last very long.

* * *

Nobody in love has good judgment; everybody
wishes, and confuses fantasy and reality.

* * *

Love letters tend to make everything sound right.

* * *

How much brain does a man need to make love
with?

* * *

Love is an unexplainable state, where there are so many things you choose, for the purpose of gratification, not to see. After satiation comes a day of reckoning. Then you really notice those things that you didn't notice before. And sometimes you make new decisions on that basis—whether to put up with it or not put up with it.

* * *

It takes a lot of work to be a lover.

* * *

Some people get an awful lot of loving out of fighting like hell for years. One of the problems of growing up is learning to be able to assess the styles different people have of getting along and loving one another.

* * *

Love is love, no matter where you find it. I really don't like the category of friendship as a separate entity, because friendship is aim-inhibited love. You love somebody and they love you, but by mutual agreement you both develop a modus operandi which protects both and still maintains the feeling relationship. Friends love each other.

* * *

When people are having trouble loving currently, it's because they have an old love that they've never given up.

* * *

One of the saddest things in life to accept is that those you love often love others more.

* * *

This psychotic state called love....

Men and Women

How long can two people hold each other without being intimate—especially when one is male and one is female?

* * *

Young women are active people—and the more they maintain their activity in a passive way, the more we think they are womanly.

* * *

Girls leave home sooner or later—and they have to be depressed to grow, even though it's hard to take seeing a woman depressed.

* * *

Every father has to seduce his daughter, in order for her to learn how to be a woman. The problems come when this seduction is so intense that she cannot give up the relationship as inappropriate and take another man for herself.

* * *

Can a woman love more than once?

* * *

A girl's a girl—sometimes you make it with her and sometimes you don't. Sometimes if you make it with her, you make a contract for a life of excitement, contentment, and difficulty.

* * *

Young ladies know when they're turned on, don't they?

* * *

Women are essentially pretty honest. They're honest at heart, but just strategic.

* * *

Nothing makes a woman more angry than to be promised something that isn't delivered.

* * *

Ask a woman a question and you'll always get an answer—but not necessarily to the question you ask.

* * *

I always marvel at the Rockettes. It's a miracle that anyone can get so many women to do the same thing at the same time.

* * *

American women don't seem prone to be mistresses, they want it for keeps. It's okay to be bait, but when she goes fishing, she wants the fish.

* * *

When can a man be his own man? Only when he can be honest and discreet with his old man.

* * *

The only thing that shakes up men is their women.

Growing, Maturing
and Sadness

Sorrow is the vitamin of growth.

* * *

The only fuel for learning is the sadness you feel from your mistakes. It's important not to waste this fuel.

* * *

People grow only around sadness. It's strange who arranged it that way, but that's the way it seems to be.

* * *

It's sad and painful not to have what you want.

* * *

Pretending that it *can* be when it *can't* is how people break their hearts.

* * *

The only thing that gets people into real trouble is *thinking*—especially when they think something that isn't so.

* * *

You have to be able to say (feeling and bearing the pang of sadness that goes with it), "I want that, but it's not for me, and I accept it." *Renunciation* is the mechanism of adaptation.

* * *

Becoming one's self is the *saddest* experience anyone can have. It means taking your feelings for the most important people to you, separating these feelings from them, then taking the idealized meanings of these feelings and introjecting them into one's self.

* * *

We're mature because we reality test; we don't continue believing what it gradually dawns on us is not true.

* * *

It's a necessary condition of human health to be able to bear what has to be borne, to be able to think what has to be thought.

* * *

Maturity is a matter of people learning to be alone together.

* * *

The more mature a relationship, the more able the two people are to give up their dependency and learn how to live alone together.

* * *

Nothing is ever mutual.

* * *

The most mature people, wherever they find themselves, are comfortable enough with themselves that they can live alone in the presence of other people. It's paradoxical, but mature object relationships are essentially relations where two or more people can live alone with each other.

* * *

In everyday life each one of you, to the extent of your maturity, lives alone. You make your own decisions, which is very lonesome. You feed yourself and look after your own physiology. Then, periodically, by mutual agreement with someone in your life, you have some human contact. And the more mature you are, the less you insist that the other person change to fit your mold, albeit one does not give up that wish altogether. Nor do others give up the idea that you ought to change to fit into their mold. But it becomes a relatively minimal matter.

* * *

You get up and get your own breakfast. If you can't get her to make the decisions for you, you have nothing left to do but make them yourself, although most couples spend an awful lot of time in trying to get each other to make up each other's mind. It all sounds paradoxical, but when you take the cool, calm, collected view of it, normality is really a very creative state.

* * *

You can only be close when you're separate.

Leaving Home

The only part of the world that is wise about the proper time to push the young out of the nest are the birds, and even they take a calculated risk. But they're willing to do it.

* * *

The only time people leave their mothers is when they're ready to go.

* * *

Every time you put a mile between a father and a daughter, her heart aches a little.

* * *

I have learned over the years that the only way a father and daughter can part is when they acknowledge how much they love each other. As long as they don't acknowledge this, as long as they "hate" each other, they stick together like glue. It happens with mothers too.

* * *

There isn't one girl in this room who hasn't crossed swords with her mother.

* * *

As long as people are mad at each other, they can't let each other go.

* * *

I've never seen anybody get mad at anybody unless he matters to her.

* * *

It's disillusioning to be mamma's fair haired boy and then find out that the rest of the world doesn't treat you that way. It can scare the life out of you.

* * *

Home is a place you can't go back to: it isn't there anymore.

Marriage

What is it that people live for? You have to find somebody of your own to live for.

* * *

People need to marry—to have peace of mind.

* * *

Even narcissistic people marry. People make all sorts of arrangements.

* * *

If people chose partners by what they are rather than what they think they are, there wouldn't be any deals. That hopefulness is what makes the deal.

* * *

Getting married is a terrific loss experience. You have to take yourself out of circulation for your own peace of mind. You shut the door behind you. You open a door too, but you don't know what's ahead. Getting married is a sad thing.

* * *

One of the blessings of human union is that it gives two people something to do.

* * *

You married fellows know how nice it is to get into bed, pat your wife's bottom, and know it will be there tomorrow.

Work

You know, nobody likes to work. It's a substitute activity for loving.

* * *

Everybody plies their trade, because this is the way they make contact with people and this is how they feel secure.

* * *

If you want to be top man you have to do the work involved, and it doesn't matter how smart you are. It might be easier to get the work done if you're smart, but the work *still* has to be done.

* * *

There's a great difference between the value you place on what you've worked for and got by your own achievement as opposed to the value you place on things you get on a silver platter. There's never much *real* personal value or self-esteem derived from anything given you on a silver platter. It can only make you feel inadequate.

* * *

You can get awfully exhausted running headlong into a wall all day long and spending all your time nursing your head instead of doing your job.

Belief

Everyone has to believe in something.

* * *

Answer to question concerning belief in God: One hundred percent of my patients believe in something.

* * *

To believe in something is a necessary psychological function. Ignorance is intolerable. There are many theories, but it still remains to be seen what the facts are.

* * *

What you *believe* and what you *know* are different things, and it's important to keep them separated for your orientation.

* * *

In the end, one goes back to his own tradition.

Thinking

It hurts to think straight.

* * *

One can get in the habit of not thinking as a defense, of not perceiving and not considering what are his perceptions and feelings about life, in order to avoid what is painful.

* * *

Nobody ever thinks *too* much.

* * *

Your mind never quits, it just keeps going on and on. Like the heart, it never stops while you're alive.

* * *

You can have definite opinions only when you don't know anything about a subject.

Decision Making

In all human affairs comes a time when you have to decide whether to fish or cut bait.

* * *

This is one of the eternal questions: How much are you going to pay for what you get?

* * *

There's nothing against acting out, as long as you know what you're doing and are willing to pay the price for it. It's always a question of the price. And the price that is most difficult to pay is the price exacted by your own conscience.

* * *

Postponement is not the way to make the most of the experience that passes under your eyes every day.

* * *

People don't like to make decisions.

* * *

I don't know of any human beings that are free—
they all have to make up their minds if they're going
to stay with Judy or go to work.

* * *

The most important task of a human being is to
make up his mind—what's for him and what's *not* for
him.

* * *

A man has a choice of doing with his life what he
wants—he can be a fool or take it seriously.

* * *

Men either take responsibility or they don't; pay for what they get or don't.

* * *

Adults are most lonely when they learn to make their own decisions, if they make them themselves.

* * *

As soon as you make a commitment, you put yourself in line for a lot of pain. It means choosing a niche for yourself and giving up all those other possibilities.

* * *

Each man wants to do what he wants to call his own. I cherish that thought very much.

* * *

If people want to do anything seriously they need all the brains they can mobilize, and most people don't have much to spare.

* * *

You can't win them all if you try: you can't win any of them if you don't.

* * *

The only reason to make a mistake is so you can learn something from it. Otherwise it's a waste of time.

* * *

Men make their decisions come hell or high water and then have to suffer for them and fall on their face many times till they can find a place for themselves in the scheme of things.

* * *

It takes a certain amount of time and exposure before you can make all the mistakes that are possible to be made.

* * *

Every time you fall on your face and fail, if you learn something from it, you progress: if you don't, you go down the drain. You're all young and maybe you have most of your failures still in the future. None of us likes to look at the failures in our lives.

* * *

Is there any other way to learn than the hard way?

Major life decisions are best made with as clear a head and heart as possible.

* * *

There are only a few choices in life: to kill yourself, go crazy, or learn to live with what you have in life.

* * *

In the depths of grief is no time to make a major life decision.

* * *

What worse thing can you do to someone you love than to die on them?

* * *

The only way one can allow oneself to be content is to *remember* the dead—and to let them be in one's memory.

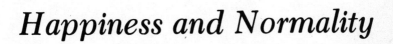

Happiness and Normality

The only happiness and security there is, is facing life as it comes and dealing with the realities.

* * *

Getting where you are is not all happiness—it costs a lot in your affective existence. You give up a lot to get what you think you want.

* * *

This is the core of living: what you feel and how you are at home with yourself.

* * *

People are happy only when their hearts and bodies are happy. Their heads don't help them a bit.

* * *

A person has to face the pain in his life in order to put it in perspective. If the shit is collecting in the barn, you've got to shovel it out. Otherwise before you know it the barn will be full and you won't be able to manage it.

* * *

What people avoid is what hurts the most.

* * *

I've always thought that some of the things people suffer most from are the things they tell themselves that are not true.

* * *

Man is his own greatest enemy, by his means of self-deception.

* * *

The reality of the world is cold and uncom-
promising. Reality doesn't change for anybody. It's
simple and clear-cut. Nothing fancy about it at all.

* * *

Reality changes so little for anybody. If reality is to
be changed, it takes an awful lot of work. Even
cooping people up in hospitals or in jails doesn't
change very much the essence of their basic nature.
Radical steps have to be taken before change can
occur.

* * *

Everything is all right as long as it's at the *right time*
with the *right people* in the *right place*.

* * *

Normality is essentially a function of where, with
whom, and when.

Miscellaneous
Remarks on Life

Where are we going and how do we get there is
something we always are working on. I'll never turn
down help from anyone.

* * *

People look after each other, if you let them.

* * *

The real pain in your life is as important to you as
the life itself. It hurts right in the middle of your heart.

* * *

Human behavior, one to the other, is not always
what it appears to be.

* * *

Following your genitals instead of your head is a dangerous game for adults.

* * *

There's one thing man has an infinite capacity for: regression.

* * *

If your heart isn't in it, you'll fail.

* * *

To a Resident: I don't think you should do anything that you don't want to do just because somebody in a position of authority said you should do it. I think you should do something that really touches the interest within you—that you want to struggle with.

* * *

Youngsters don't understand sex in old people.

* * *

People *do* get shocked into reconsiderations.

* * *

Willpower is a wonderful thing. The only trouble with willpower is the unaccounted unconscious factors that interfere with it from time to time.

* * *

You can't take anybody else's guilt, you can just have your own.

* * *

People are people. They all have to grow up and face issues and deal with them in some way. The first thing they deal with is control of their own body and all the feelings in it; then, how to get other people to help them with their feelings. They have to work out equitable distances to live and love with people.

* * *

There's nothing more disappointing to a human being than false hopes.

* * *

Everyone's either mad, sad, or afraid.

* * *

You'd be surprised how many people look good all day at work but go home at night and cry into their pillows.

* * *

It's hard for a man to say he doesn't know.

* * *

Who can tell anybody anything?

* * *

You can tell people what you think, but they don't have to believe you.

* * *

The second *no* means *yes*. More than one *no* indicates ambivalence.

* * *

Taking over is a two-person proposition:
someone has to want to, and someone has to allow it.

* * *

Nebishes are very powerful; they control whole
families for years.

* * *

A little schmaltz never hurt anyone.

* * *

You can always find something to beat somebody
over the head with.

* * *

It's interesting how one can always get a job as a dishwasher, anywhere in the world.

* * *

Never idealize anybody; they all stink.

* * *

This is the kind of stuff people live.

* * *

Life is really simple, but we don't let ourselves have it.

On Therapy
and in Therapy

I don't know very many "ordinary people." I never treated anyone who didn't need treatment.

* * *

We all have a load; and we have to work with the load we've got, with the way we are. We could all use some time to think about ourselves. The routine time is fifty minutes, but that's ten minutes of getting started, twenty minutes of therapeutic alliance, ten minutes of work, and ten minutes of preparation to get back to reality.

* * *

There is no human being who can resist a helping situation. He'll always go there—like a fly to honey.

* * *

Patients do not quit helping situations. They get thrown out, but they don't quit.

* * *

A therapist is a kind of service man. There are so many things a patient can want to use you for—and if you can swallow your own ideas of how things *should* be, you can perform a real service.

* * *

On "Supportive Therapy": Therapy is therapy— talking to the patient about what matters to him, no matter at what pace he can take it.

* * *

As long as you take the position of talking to a person about what matters to him, then he can feel secure. Someone cares enough and is concerned enough about him to work with him and listen.

* * *

Talk with regressed patients about what really matters to them.

* * *

The only way you can put a floor under a patient is by getting him to talk about what is most important to him at that moment.

* * *

We must insist on talking to patients only about what they actually experience. In other words, go right through the defenses, rather than lose our efforts in helping them strengthen their already strong defenses. The only thing we really deal with in our relationships with patients is their actual life experience—not the stock they came from, their heredity, their genes, their biological propensities to growth. All we deal with is their reaction to their life experience; how much of it they integrated and how much of it isn't integrated; how much they can handle and how much they can't handle, but have to postpone or avoid or deny. And the more infantile the personality, the more they handle by avoidance.

* * *

We must help the patient to acknowledge, bear, and put into perspective his feelings.

* * *

Everything is a vehicle for therapeutic interchange; and the closer it comes to the patient, the more of his interest it gets, the better—whether his interest is in the service of resistance or not. You're a talking doctor.

* * *

In response to a resident's request for advice regarding what to say to a patient: We all have the same question and problem, and I follow a very simple rule: If it's comfortable for me to say it, then it is the right thing, the right time, and the right way to say it.

* * *

Go after what the patient feels and cannot do himself. Help him to acknowledge what he cannot bear himself, and stay with him until he can stand it.

* * *

As a psychiatrist, your job is to help the patient stand his pain, and this is directly contrary to the rest of the medical profession.

* * *

You can't cure appendicitis by putting salve on your big toe.

* * *

We do what they did in the twenties to osteomyelitis: open up the wound and clean out the pus, as painful as this is, and then keep open the wound and let it heal from the bottom up.

* * *

Laymen often think that the best way to deal with any difficult situation is *not* to deal with it—to forget it. But you and I have the experience that the only way you can forget is to remember.

* * *

No therapy is comfortable, because it involves dealing with pain. But there's one comfortable thought: that two people sharing pain can bear it easier than one.

* * *

The most important therapeutic element we have is empathy. Be empathic—just long enough.

* * *

If you can't sit with the patient until he can feel it in his own body then you're in the wrong business.

* * *

Find out what the heart says, and where in the body the feelings are.

* * *

Don't get involved in judgments; concentrate on working through feelings.

* * *

The way to deal with someone who lies is to get to his feelings, because feelings never lie.

* * *

Keep the patient responsible: *You* were there; you did it. What did you do and what did you think while you were living your life?

* * *

You help a patient take responsibility by making him responsible for everything he says.

* * *

Loan him your strength in making him responsible for thinking for himself and making his own decision.

* * *

You have to respect his adulthood. To do this you have to treat him with respect and approach him on his highest level of function. Don't take away from him what he has, or you'll foster regression.

* * *

In answer to a resident's question as to how long to tell a patient he will need therapy: As long as it takes.

* * *

Resident: Can you let the patient know that you want him to get better and pass a developmental hurdle?
Semrad: Always, but never for me.

* * *

Be calm as you go after just the facts.

* * *

The technique of therapy can be to go over and over the facts—to pick up the cues omitted from consideration at the time.

* * *

Investigate, investigate, investigate.

* * *

Whenever you don't know what to do: investigate.

* * *

Can you stand to sit with him and take the initiative and insist on the facts?

* * *

Who's doing what to whom?

* * *

The patient knows what's happened in his life, what bugs him, what hurts.

* * *

What's important is when, with whom, under what circumstance, and for what purpose.

* * *

Stay with the person's experience, and don't get seduced by some of the fancy concepts you've heard about.

* * *

If you stare and stare at the data, it occasionally sends a message that was not brought to your associations before.

* * *

The only truth you have is your patient. And the only thing that interferes with that truth is your own perception. You may not be free to observe what is there to be observed, chiefly because it evokes feelings in you that are so troublesome that you quit looking. This is one of the big things Charcot told Freud over and over again.

* * *

Be firm, fair, and understanding. Hold the reins in one hand and a lump of sugar in the other.

* * *

The only insight he needs is that you mean what you say.

* * *

Don't manipulate or connive—just let the people work it out.

* * *

You have to be very careful with what you say to people—they might believe you!

* * *

Don't let a patient hypothesize. Whenever he guesses or supposes, go after the specific details of the experience so you can help the patient recall what he has repressed in order to avoid.

* * *

If you think about where the patient is stuck in his life and what issues he's failed to work out and integrate so that he could continue his development, you'll have a much greater chance of therapeutic success than if you just try to pin a label on him or call him a diagnostic name.

* * *

I don't think the patient cares about the diagnosis. He's more concerned with what he can or cannot do.

* * *

We jump right into wondering about the genesis of character, but pay too little attention to why the patient could function yesterday the way he was, but can't function today.

* * *

Concerning "Direct Analysis": Rosen had the fantasy that he was directly communicating with the patient's unconscious. Now, more experienced observers watching him work were not so sure that he wasn't doing anything except talking dirty to another

human being to get the human being's attention.
When he got on the patient's back there was no escape
for the patient except to pay attention to him, and
what would happen was that the acute regression
would give way to the patient's return to what he was
capable of doing before he regressed.

* * *

An intellectual explanation can keep a patient
from remembering what was really important *the
way it was*.

* * *

To get anywhere with patients you have to go the
affective route.

* * *

A man's either scared, mad, or sad. If he's talking
about anything else, he's being superficial.

* * *

It's hard to look at the bottom of a well and see what's there.

* * *

The only way to get through avoidance behavior is through the affect. The technique is to talk of emotions and show the patient that he has them.

* * *

Anything short of the patient talking about the actual circumstances of his life is resistance, and you don't go along with resistance.

* * *

Nothing makes an interviewer more impotent than dealing with the resistance of a patient, especially when that resistance is based on real pain. Every time you touch it, the patient hurts.

* * *

Resistance is universal. As a matter of fact, as far as analysis is concerned, by the time the patient stops saying *no* the analysis is over.

* * *

Your own associations can be very helpful if presented in the spirit of inquiry and help.

* * *

One has to keep issues open so the patient can be free to think about them.

* * *

I don't like this term *point out*, because it implies that you've made up your mind and he has to take it. I would rather ask, ask, ask, and let him give you the data. Use the data you get to present to him and further ask. Present your conclusions to the patient as observations on which he can comment. People don't value anything except what they make for themselves.

* * *

One way to keep issues open is to keep going into the specifics.

* * *

The things that work are all worked out. It's the things that don't to which we have to address ourselves. So talking about anything short of problems is a waste of time.

* * *

The most important thing, the thing that makes the difference, the thing we as psychiatrists are dealing in, is love and humanity.

* * *

You've got to love your patients.

* * *

It's hard to say no to yourself sometimes. It's easy to want to love the patient and not to keep at the work.

* * *

It's nice to flirt with a pretty girl; but it isn't therapy.

* * *

Nothing is more difficult for a young doctor, in countertransference, than to find a patient charming. It interferes with his objectivity.

* * *

A little love can go a long way.

* * *

How do you motivate people to get back into the world? By letting them fall in love with you. How else?

* * *

It's big trouble when you encourage a girl to fall in love with you and then don't help her work it through and give you up.

* * *

Use the transference feelings of love as an affective link to the person in the past from whom it is transfered.

* * *

With transference love, don't shut the love off, but aim to redirect the love *back*, to grieve what could not be fulfilled; redirect it *forward* to where it may be expressed appropriately; and accept the reality of the inappropriate expression of the love within the therapy.

* * *

Can you stand the rationalization that you can learn something if you call it research? Then the focus shifts from trying to cure the patient to trying to understand him, and only then can you help the patient.

* * *

Don't get set on curing her, but on understanding her. If you understand, and she understands what you understand, then cure will follow naturally.

* * *

One of the main functions of anger is it allows one to say what he really thinks. He may take it back later when he cools down, but it's important to remember what he said and to deal with it, because that's where the heart of the feeling is.

* * *

We don't think often, how useful it can be for somebody to be able to go where he can get mad as hell—and nothing happens. People are willing to pay a lot of money for that.

* * *

Somebody's got to be in control, and that's you. And if you can control yourself and not make promises you can't keep or threats you can't carry out, you won't get into trouble, because the patient will be secure.

* * *

If you can get the patient to say it with his mouth, then he won't have to do it with his muscle. The fist may be aimed at you, but unless you move it won't come your way. If you invite it, you'll get it.

* * *

If you get a dog in a corner and keep baiting him, chances are he'll eventually try and bite you.

* * *

There is only acting out if someone has given permission for it.

* * *

The natural antidote to anxiety is action, and the kind of action useful to an individual is constructive action. So if you give him something constructive to do, you relieve his anxiety and possibly help him at the same time.

* * *

People in the process of growth and development experience a terrific frustration and pain, especially when it is telescoped into a short period of time.

* * *

It's easy to find out the important persons in someone's life by talking to him. It's not so easy to find out the idealized meanings of these important persons, because these are so much a part of one and syntonic with one.

* * *

Weaning is a very sad experience for everybody, whether it's weaning from the breast itself, or whether it's weaning from some substitute of the breast. The first loss is giving up something that one has had, and it becomes the prototype of all later mourning experience. It's very sad to allow yourself to remember something that has been—that is no more.

* * *

One of the hardest things for people to get used to is to allow people to come and go in their life, and to do the necessary affective work, namely, taking their investment from what they had before, putting it back into themselves, and then reinvesting it into something or someone else. This is the hardest work that goes into the whole phenomenon of growth and development. Growth in terms of self-differentiation and self-maturation is a very sad process.

* * *

Spontaneous recoveries are hard for us to know much about, because we seldom study them.

* * *

One hears a lot about miserable lives. The question is, What makes the difference between being miserable in an adaptive way and being miserable in a nonadaptive way?

* * *

Analysis of the transference relationship, to put it in ordinary terms, means that the analysand lets his analyst die for him. In essence he says to the analyst: "It's been nice, it's been terrible. It's been wonderful, but I don't need you anymore. You go your way and I'll go my way." But very few analyses come to that point of natural conclusion. This is a leap right out of life, as when the developing child can say, "Well, Dad had a good life. The only trouble he had was with Mother: the only joy he had was with Mother. They had a hell of a time together, but he's had it. We'll put him on the hill, mourn him, and go about our business." In some sense it sounds cold and unfeeling, but this is the process that *somebody* started. Some believe that it is under some organized auspices, to which I could not attest one way or the other. But I observe it.

* * *

You have to keep the *old* alive long enough to peter out and not just be cut off. The decathexis-recathexis process is universal.

* * *

All's fair in love, war, and therapy.

* * *

The best novels I hear are on the couch—they capture everything that's on paper.

*Case Conference Comments
to the Patient*

I don't know how it is with you. That's what I want to find out.

* * *

What's in your life *for you*?

* * *

You must talk only about what really matters to you.

* * *

You need your sleep, but you have to settle the important issues in your life to enable you to sleep.

* * *

As you study this feeling, what does it tell you?

* * *

Don't you acknowledge the truth of your feelings?

* * *

Don't you believe what you feel? It's pretty bad if a man can't believe in himself.

* * *

Can you prove it? If you can prove it, I'll believe it.

* * *

Come clean! You know, I have a feeling about you. And when an old man has a feelin', he has a feelin'.

* * *

Responsibility must be merited. Like love, it can't be given away.

* * *

Are you willing to pay the price for what you want?

* * *

Get yourself a good woman and work for her.

* * *

How did you make him do that to you?

* * *

What are you going to do for yourself?

* * *

Case Conference Comments
to the
Therapist and Staff

Now we have a chance to ply our trade—to help her do what she can't do herself.

* * *

You have to be fair, firm, understanding, and not take any bunk from him.

* * *

When he's in treatment, we first have to get him over all the doctors' help he's already gotten.

* * *

This is what makes the difference, the *tissues* of the persons involved, not the fancy thoughts upstairs. He's living a real honest human experience, with every tissue of his being.

* * *

What does his body tell him?

* * *

I don't care about what *you* feel. What does *he* feel?

* * *

To bring her head and her heart together is the problem.

* * *

Nobody's ever empty, doctor. They're full of something they sometimes don't want you to see, or to see themselves.

* * *

Acknowledging the feelings and reality of her body is overwhelming her mind with guilt.

* * *

There's no doubt that the genesis of her present
situation is in her development, but therapeutically
that's not the issue. The issue is the overwhelming
pain she can't face right now.

* * *

She just doesn't want to know what she knows,
because it's all so sad.

* * *

What's going on in his living and loving that he
can't stand to look at?

* * *

He may reject the therapist because he cannot
tolerate what he begins to feel.

* * *

When you talk about what's important, the patient will always tear.

* * *

Once he showed his tears, that was enough for me. I respect the autonomic nervous system to show feelings like I respect few other things.

* * *

In a conference about the treatment of psychotic patients: You wonder if they ever did anything very interesting in their lives, or whether it was all emptiness and failure. . . . Well, you can bet your bottom dollar about one thing they did: once upon a time they loved somebody.

* * *

When you feel that you matter to somebody, then you can't help but feel loved; and when you feel loved, you don't have to be crazy.

* * *

After an interview with a psychotic patient: He didn't disorganize, because I was persistent and kept him at work. I let him know I meant business, and he was reassured and settled down.

* * *

I just acknowledged that she was hurting about something that mattered a great deal to her. She was able to acknowledge it, and it wasn't so bad. I also said, "You must have loved him very much." She said, "Yes." And then she said, "Well, what can I expect from my therapy?" I said, "Nothing but work." And this was very consoling to her.

* * *

From a letter to a private therapist who had sent a patient for consultation: He has little experience bearing his sadness, and is warding it off through depressive activities.... I asked him to tell me what he wants—"a crutch," he says.... I told him to return to you and level with you about the life issues that matter to him most.... The initiative falls to his therapist to help him acknowledge, bear, and put these issues into perspective.... You must help him come to terms with his limitations and decide what he will do in his life that is consonant with his talents.

* * *

The only kind of worthwhile addiction I can think of for this patient is her therapist.

* * *

The basic decision a therapist has to make in a case like this is whether he's going to stick it out doing things *with* her, or whether he's going to resort to doing things *to* her.

* * *

You can't just aid and abet his defenses—they didn't work. That's why he got here.

* * *

A therapist who is not oriented to going after what the patient avoids could sit with this woman for five years and get nowhere.

* * *

Do you think you can be the man he can love until he can love himself?

* * *

The hole in his heart is the denial that he's like his father. They can't love each other because they're so much alike.

* * *

Does she love him enough to let him go?

* * *

Her biggest problem is that she doesn't want to live in the world as it is.

* * *

Bright red apple, wrong orchard.

* * *

What is his tradition? Everybody has one, you know.

* * *

Negativity in mourning is entirely a defense against the pain of being left. It's the *love* she misses.

* * *

His parents are still an important factor; like an old dog who looks dead, every once in a while a piece of him jumps.

* * *

In reference to ward decisions regarding a patient: Somebody's got to take the position of making decisions and following through, and then has to be willing to be the scapegoat if the decisions don't work out.

* * *

You're his therapist, not his administrator. You just study the *no's* that the administrator gives him.

* * *

As she forms a relationship, her resistance to the transference work will be her sexual feelings, which will have to be dealt with. She'll have to learn to *acknowledge*, *bear*, and *put into perspective* her feelings. The work can be a corrective ego experience.

* * *

When a doctor is a patient, most important is that you don't want to harm his position as a patient.

* * *

If I were young and full of vim and vigor, I would take on this case with no commitment to cure him, but rather to learn how a young man can sacrifice his whole life in a death struggle with his mother; to see how people really work and can do this to each other.

* * *

Dying is a very serious matter, because you can do it only once. Nobody knows if an afterlife is a fact or a belief, because no one's come back to discuss it. If she wants to believe there's an afterlife, that's her decision. As psychiatrists, we're interested in making sure she knows the difference between belief and fact.

* * *

It may seem unusual, but life *is* that way. We didn't start it and we won't end it. We can only aid and abet people to get along with some degree of equanimity and purpose.

* * *

My favorite question is, What do you really want to do? It's a question I've thought out over the years. And it's important, because it involves how he wants to spend all the years of his life.

* * *

Why should you try to decide whether his decisions are best for him? Why don't you leave that up to him? He has to decide if his decisions are what he wants for himself. You should just take the questioning end, and help him to decide for himself.

* * *

How long term do I see him? As long as it takes. That's like asking how long it takes to grow up.

* * *

Time means nothing in this business.

Psychodynamics

All defenses are forms of self-deception, whether by avoidance or postponement.

* * *

With neurotics, the primary defense is repression. With psychotics, the primary defense is avoidance. They're two different ways of maintaining equilibrium. Repression is just a postponement—being strong enough to say to yourself, Not now, I'll deal with it later. But in avoidance, you sacrifice what you have, in order not to have to deal with what is overwhelming to you.

* * *

The purpose of depression is to get *somebody else* to do something they're not doing.

* * *

Depression is an aggressive act to one's objects.

* * *

Depression can be a defense against sadness.

* * *

Chronicity or staying in a psychotic episode means that there is a decision to be made about the objects in one's current life.

* * *

All chronicity is, is not solving the original regression and the factors involved in it.

* * *

Chronicity is always evidence that the first precipitating incident of the first regression has never been adequately dealt with.

* * *

Chronicity follows when the precipitating factor in the original regression has not been worked through and resolved. This is what the therapist must go for.

* * *

Chronicity is the result of not having resolved the first major regression, and always the same element that precipitated this first regression is revived and precipitates further regression.

* * *

Preadolescent masturbation is very much a general body phenomenon. Adult sexuality is a cooperative endeavor. It's fortunate that people get into that psychotic state called love so that no one pays attention to who's doing what to whom.

* * *

Sexuality is a peculiar human experience. There's nothing like the first time—ever. All that emotion and feeling. It just never happens again. Whenever you awaken a new experience, it's hard to duplicate it. Especially when it's a gratification—it's like the first time you had vanilla ice cream.

* * *

Displacements don't solve anything because they're not for real. That's the only reason we're able to help anyone: because the neurotic and psychotic positions are less acceptable than the real McCoy.

* * *

Ambivalence toward an important object can keep one glued to him.

* * *

One of the purposes of a psychotic episode is to find out what one feels.

* * *

If you don't solve something the first time, the ego has the tendency to go back over and over again in an attempt to resolve it and set things straight.

* * *

The hope of the repetition compulsion: that next time will be better!

* * *

When you speak of ego and ego capacities, you are really talking about a person's experience in all aspects of his existence; whether it's in relation to other people, or whether it's in relation to his own body; whether it's in relation to getting other people to do things for him, or in relation to maintaining himself and managing himself as a person so that he can stay in some more or less gratifying relationship with another human being. No matter what kind of genetic stock the ego comes from, it still has these very basic areas of growth and development to master to some semblance of perfection that often is loosely called maturity. It has to develop behaviors to preserve itself in some semblance of equanimity and psychic constancy, it has to develop capacities to get other people to do things for it, and it has to learn about self-sacrifice: what you give up of yourself in order to keep other people around.

* * *

The ego, at all times and under all conditions, functions as a symphony; although you sometimes can't hear the clarinets from the basses.

* * *

Establishing ego boundaries is a decathexis-recathexis process.

* * *

The way an ego functions in what you call disease is just an exaggeration of the way it functions in health. Healthy neurotics are never a clinical problem. They go about their business in their own mild anxiety, live a lifetime of relative equanimity and satisfaction, and have no need for treatment. But if certain things happen and their anxiety gets beyond a certain point, then they present themselves for help, and at that point they become clinical problems. The young lady who has a headache when she doesn't want to go out with somebody, gradually *uses* headaches, which she suffers and has great distress and incapacity from. She may be diagnosed as a hysteric, but only when it becomes exaggerated to the point that it keeps her relatively nonfunctional. It's the same thing with manic depressive states or affective disorders. There are periods of manic activity that are useful and important and socially compatible. Without them there wouldn't be a life of the party, you know. It's always a question of time, place, and person. Normality is essentially a function of where, with whom, and when.

* * *

The only active ego reintegrating agent is positive affect: love, or positive transference.

* * *

A functioning ego split is necessary to interrupt character syntonicity.

* * *

The only use of projection is to force *responsibility sharing* out of objects.

* * *

Preoedipal problems, two-people relationship problems, are essentially survival problems: so much depends on the presence of the other person, and unless the other person complies, there is no survival. By the time you get into oedipal, three-people relationship problems, the ego is more mature and more able to postpone action. Oedipal problems are essentially erotic problems. The difference is the problems of survival versus the problems of sharing.

* * *

It wasn't so long ago that nobody had heard of such a thing as an unconscious. Today, it's as common as southern fried chicken. Nobody questions it. That is, if he does any thinking at all. But it's still phenomenal.

Symptoms and Signs

Symptoms are solutions.

* * *

Think about the purpose of the symptoms: what does the symptom do for the person?

* * *

Tears never lie in a male.

* * *

Wise guy behavior has the theme of having fun at others' expense.

* * *

I don't have any more interest in hallucinations and delusions than I would in a fever. I don't care about the fever, but about what's going on to cause it. Don't get me wrong, fever is interesting for people interested in research on fever. But what are you going to do with this guy, help him or make him an academic study?

* * *

There are reminders of the oral period in everyone. Kissing is a remnant of the oral period, and I don't think anyone in this room would want to abolish it.

* * *

Character behavior is unthinking behavior.

* * *

Panic is the signal that something is going on in your life that needs attention.

On Specific Diagnoses

What does it really mean to be schizophrenic? It means one is at a disadvantage.

* * *

It's expensive to be crazy.

* * *

Being schizophrenic is not only expensive, it's the most dangerous illness you can have, because it gives everyone the license to try out all their ideas on you, to try and change you.

* * *

The word *schizophrenia* makes doctors forget everything they've learned about working with people, and makes them search frantically for something magic. I've been in this business for a long time, and I've never yet found any magic. And I've done a lot of looking, believe me.

* * *

Psychotic patients are no different than we are, just a little crazier. And if we don't precipitate a fight, they won't, because chances are they're more scared than we are.

* * *

As soon as someone says the word *schizophrenia*, everyone jumps, and no one wants to work with the patient anymore. They either want to leave the patient alone or do something *to* him, rather than thinking of working *with* him on the issues in his life.

* * *

Schizophrenics are very strong. They live a long time. To get them to change is no easy matter; to give up the position they hold for a position of normality, which is an uncomfortable state that involves making one's own decisions, making one's own living, and making sure that what you do is in some measure equitable with the feelings of other people.

* * *

Regarding schizophrenic inpatients: I haven't met a patient here who hasn't had some idea of what pain in their life they're avoiding. And the thing is that they cannot bear that pain and they go through all sorts of antics to get somebody to make it better, which looks very infantile. But if they can bear it themselves, they don't have to be so infantile. I wouldn't analyze anybody for avoidance problems; for not being able to bear the pain of their life and the issues around which it centers. I would help them develop some structure so that they could acknowledge and bear it and put it into perspective.

* * *

Catatonics are living out the old saying, If you don't know what to do, don't do anything.

* * *

One thing I learned early in my career about manic patients is that I can't outmanipulate them, because they're so good at it they can beat me every time— they're expert. The only better manipulator is a psychopath.

* * *

Neurasthenia is the art of studied ineptitude.

* * *

You deal with the neurasthenic by appealing to his narcissism: what does he want for himself, and is he willing to pay the price for it?

* * *

Narcissistic regression is an attempt to avoid the pain of the sadness in one's life.

* * *

A borderline is a person who looks like a neurotic, but who has much more infantile, narcissistic ways of dealing with the world.

* * *

That's the borderline feature of her personality—that she focuses on hypothesis elaboration, rather than on reality testing.

* * *

Follow affective cues, and don't be so inactive with a borderline.

* * *

People with character neuroses are always doing something at the wrong time, in the wrong place, and with the wrong people.

* * *

The royal road to being successful in therapy with a character disorder is to be available to him as a love object and to be tested by him without bashing him in the face.

* * *

The rule in treating character disorders is: look, smell, and listen, but never touch or taste.

* * *

A severe character disorder may become schizophrenic if the patient doesn't get into good therapeutic hands.

* * *

With anal-compulsive, passive-aggressively defended people who are really digging their heels in and won't budge, you have to work with them and take them through the stages from *I don't know* to *I can't* to *I won't*, and show them how they are using their defenses.

* * *

Alcoholics are notorious for loving their little girls. And what's more, little girls love their alcoholic fathers, even if their mothers can't stand them. They go on marrying one alcoholic after another.

* * *

All hysteria is, is not taking the responsibility for adult sexuality.

* * *

Unless someone can take the responsibility, the hysterical young lady will sit you out every time.

* * *

The normal distribution of hysteria in the female population makes them interesting people. When it gets too much, it's a pain in the neck.

* * *

Hysterics may take on what you give them; they may be fluid in personality—the therapist must know what to give them and follow it through to understand its meaning.

* * *

It's amazing the amount of repression that is available to the hysterical character. They don't see, hear, or feel—they just seduce everything in sight.

* * *

Dodging adult responsibility is the symptom par excellence of hysteria—even to the point of losing a function.

* * *

With a hysterical female, everything or anything is okay, as long as *you* take the responsibility. One can use this therapeutically.

* * *

Intellectual people you approach through their intellect, knowing full well that that's not what they want, and that they'll eventually get tired of it and give you the signal that they want to talk about what really matters to them. Then take the signal.

* * *

Hypochondriasis is when someone says, If you don't love me for what I am, at least give me some

---

sympathy—if not for all of me, at least for my liver.
Treat me like when I had the mumps.

* * *

And so often, when you get to know a patient, they
lose their diagnosis, you know.

Drugs, Druggers
and Hospitals

When you take poison, sooner or later you get poisoned. And all drugs are poison.

* * *

Drugs separate the mind from the body.

* * *

On phenothiazines: They're chemical straitjackets.

* * *

How can a person deal with the problems of his life when he's drugged?

* * *

If they have to get addicted, I would rather have them addicted to psychotherapy than to drugs.

* * *

I don't object to the use of pills. I just want to be sure why they're given.

* * *

I've never seen a group that is more hopeful or willing to believe in magic than the endocrine people. They think if they can just find the right *juice*, life will be an endless pleasure.

* * *

We're in an era where treatment is not popular. We're in a manipulation era.

* * *

When the emphasis goes to drugs, restrictions, and controls, then love goes out the window and the patients lose out.

* * *

Management includes restrictions: and half of restriction is punishment, the other half, seduction.

* * *

Giving structure is the same as taking charge in a benevolent way.

* * *

Plans are a dime a dozen. Making them work is the payoff.

* * *

A comment to a treatment-planning team: Who's gonna be Poppa, who's gonna be Momma, and who's gonna be Uncle Miltie?

* * *

Hospitals never did anything for anybody. It's the *people* in the hospitals that are the active therapeutic agents.

* * *

When you use a hospital for any more than riding over a crisis and attaching to a therapist, then you're not running a hospital, you're running a hotel.

* * *

Did you ever hear of people accomplishing anything by staying in a hotel except getting into more trouble? That's why the hotel business flourishes!

Residents and Training

Comment to the senior staff and chief residents:
Each man that comes here is an investment in our
future, and we should treat him as such.

* * *

We choose mules for residents; people who are not
too sadistic, who aren't pushovers, and who think for
themselves.

* * *

We choose residents who are not sadistic and who
are comfortable with their own passivity.

* * *

The different points of view here is the strength of
our program. It forces the resident to choose for
himself and be his own man. If that means he has to
go through a lot of pain and suffering, that's all right
with me.

* * *

I seldom worry about the feelings of the residents; I worry about the feelings of the patients.

* * *

The first year, the experience and learning grows from the seat of your pants. You've got to read the patient, the original textbook, and not a book.

* * *

The patient is the only textbook we require.

* * *

At the first-year resident level, you have no business worrying about money. Your job is to learn your trade as best you can. If you learn your trade well, someone will come up with the money.

* * *

Comment to the chief residents: Help them survive the ordeal of doing something that seems to them impossible. We train, we don't educate.

* * *

You need to help the resident keep working and not go through these periods of being as stymied as the patient. You have to help the resident *not to go dead*.

* * *

He's like any resident. They ask, but they don't want anyone to make up their minds for them.

* * *

To provide education for this field isn't easy, especially when you're dealing with a group of men who already know more than they can use.

* * *

Your job as chief is to see that the patients get good care and to train the residents to do this. Take care of them and teach them their trade.

* * *

Comment to the chief: It is not your job to kiss asses. It *is* your job to set limits about the appropriate treatment of a patient and to point out to a resident that he's fucking up.

* * *

It's the chief's job to be covered with shit, but to keep one eye open and clear so that he at least can tell where it's coming from and what has to be cleaned up.

* * *

I hope you will take away with you what you found valuable, use it, and pass it on. As for the rest, throw it away!

Therapists

What a hell of a way to make a living: to prostitute yourself, make love, and effect separations for money.

* * *

We doctors can't stand death. We can't stand the awful reality that something *doesn't exist*.

* * *

We're physicians. We're supposed to know about these problems.

* * *

There are very attractive female bodies with "male brains." And vice versa, you know. There are an awful lot of nice guys who think like women, you know. Some of them make good psychoanalysts, because once they make their peace with their passivity, they don't have to do anything but listen.

*   *   *

Of course in the ideal private practice you'll only have patients that come to *you*. They'll pay you enough to buy your wife's new hat and Chanukah gifts, and you'll get the gratification of knowing they come to you every week to do the thinking they're too lazy to do on their own. I know I'm burlesquing this a little; I'm not as blind as I look.

*   *   *

A psychiatrist can't expect to get his narcissistic supplies from his patients. He has to look elsewhere for gratification, like taking an extra helping of flapjacks on Sunday morning.

*   *   *

The ability to share desperation is what makes a therapist. One becomes a therapist because of his own desperation.

* * *

We're just service people, and how to define our service task is our biggest problem.

* * *

We're just big messes trying to help bigger messes, and the only reason we can do it is that we've been through it before and have survived.

* * *

One of the most common countertransference pains that the psychiatrist has to get used to is the pain in the neck displaced upward. Because after all, we're dealing with sick people. People as they are, are the psychiatrist's ever present countertransference problem. When it ends, I don't know. I haven't lived that long.

Writing

How can you write from the bottom of your heart if you haven't explored it yourself?

* * *

To be a good writer you have to do the same thing as to be a good therapist—to understand all about yourself and to be able to accept yourself as a person.

* * *

One of the greatest obstacles in clinical writing is the fantasy, I don't know enough to write.

Personal Comments

Ewalt says that he was brought up with horses and I was with mules.

* * *

If I weren't an optimistic guy, I would have quit this business thirty years ago. I got it from Whitehorn.* I didn't understand what he was doing half the time, but I tried to do what he told me, and I could see that it mattered to the patient.

* * *

My main interest is to kibitz and learn.

* * *

* During his final residency year, at the McLean Hospital, Dr. Semrad worked with and learned from Dr. John Whitehorn, who later succeeded Adolph Meyer as Phipps Professor of Psychiatry at the Johns Hopkins Medical School.

I'm always willing to learn something I don't know anything about. That's one reason I've been around residents for the last twenty-five years.

* * *

Everybody wants his original gratification, and it's a sad day when it is no more. It goes on and it goes on and it goes on until the day you kick the bucket. We sometimes debate here with our patients to separate them from their Mama. And everybody says, "Get him away from his mother," except me, who says, "It's the only Mama he's got. When he can leave her, which is not easy, he will!"

There is not one of you in this room who has not put some effort into tearing away from the original family unit, for whatever it was. It wasn't all peaches and cream, or all a rose garden, but you remember when you went away, how, as time went along, you got awfully anxious to go back. And after the celebration was over, they grabbed you, and took you and gave you whatever your favorite things were. Then one day, two days, three days, and you see that it isn't any different than the day you left it, and you're ready to return to what you were doing. You couldn't stand it another month, two months. Has this ever happened to you?

This goes on all the time in everyday life, and the hardest thing to get used to is to allow people to come and go out of your life; to do the work of decathecting what *was* and recathecting what *is* available to you. And as chronology goes on, there's not so much available to you any more. Something you'll notice, and you probably already have, is that one of the things that *is* available, is your work! And you work, and you work, and you work. You're always thinking of a new project: investing in activities that you have control of and you can master. How many wives can you have, you know? Most of us can't support one. There comes a time when your kids start doing the same things, and you find one day that the only usefulness you have is to be a resource, like a filling station attendant—to make sure there is plenty of gas, so that when somebody decides to drop in, you're available. And then off we go again.

It's not a one-sided proposition. Parents have as much trouble letting go as youngsters have about going. I don't know how many of you still have your mother living, but if you have, then you know she still thinks of you as the day you dropped out of sight— that primarily you're still the sixteen-year-old boy. In spite of all the degrees you may have, all the publications that you have, and all that you have achieved, you're her boy. This came to my attention very crucially one day. I was a sophomore in medical school, and one of my aunts was having a baby. My mother was not a midwife, but when anybody had trouble, there was my mother. I had just had my first introduction to obstetrics and the mythology of mother-child relationships: that you don't really need to play the piano to have a musically inclined child, and so forth. Well, I brought this information, in discussing my aunt, to my mother. She listened patiently, and interestedly. She just had a third-grade education, you know. When I got through, she said: "Well, Elvin, you're an educated man; you think one thing, and I'll think what I want to." And that was the end of the conversation.

* * *

Resident: What do you think helped build your capacity to help people bear intense feelings of loneliness and loss?

Semrad: A life of sorrow, and the opportunity that some people gave me to overcome it and deal with it.